I Love You

How to Say "I Love You"
in 99 Different Languages.

BRG Publishing
Minneapolis

Published by
BRG Publishing
a division of
Austin Industries, Inc.
Minneapolis, Minnesota 55403

Questions or comments, please call (612) 870-4711.

ISBN 0-9661144-1-8

Manufactured in the United States of America.

Fall 1997

10 9 8 7 6 5 4 3 2 1

Preface

The words "I Love You" are probably the three most beautiful words in all the world. They are at once completely understandable, needing no explanation.

In creating this book, we are mindful of the importance of these three words. And we have sought to provide for individuals who care deeply for one another, a means of expressing that feeling in more than one way, 99 different ways, to be exact.

In this book you will find an almost inexhaustible supply of different ways to say these three words. And as you use each phrase with your special person, you can give it your own special meaning and emphasis.

Our research has turned up 99 different ways of saying "I Love You," each from a different country. Some countries, of course, share their language with another country, Mexico and Spain, for example, France and Belgium, Portugal and Brazil. In far more cases, however, each country has its own language. For the sake of simplicity, we have selected the most common language from each.

We hope you will want to use many of these languages, and will eventually use every one of them. You will quickly see that we give you a phonetic way to say each phrase, so that you will get them very close to exactly right. When you plan to use them, practice a bit. Not only will you have fun doing so, but eventually you will come off as a thoroughly sophisticated traveler of the world.

So, here is the international "I Love You," to be used in times both serious and light-hearted, but always with a very special and deeply-felt meaning.

Afghanistan

Pronunciation

Mahn Ah-she-g Tow-ahm

Algeria

Pronunciation

Mahn Ah-she-g Tow-ahm

Angola

Ay-oh Ah-moe Voe-say

Argentina

Pronunciation

Tay Ah-moe

Armenia

Kay-zee Gay Sir-ram

Australia

I Love You

Austria

Eeek Leebah Deek

Bahamas

I Love You

Bangladesh

Pronunciation

Ah-me Thoe-mock-eye Bah-low Bah-she

Belgium

Pronunciation

Sheh Tehm

Bolivia

Pronunciation

Tay Ah-moe

Brazil

Pronunciation

Ay-oh Ah-moe Voe-say

Britain

Pronunciation

I Love You

Burundi

Pronunciation

Nah-coo-Pen-dah

Cambodia

Pronunciation

Kin-ohm Sir-lahn Knee-rock

Canada

Pronunciation

I Love You

Cape Verde

Pronunciation

Ay-oh Ah-moe Voe-say

Chad

Pronunciation

Ahna heh-Beck

Chile

Pronunciation

Tay Ah-moe

China

Pronunciation

Woll - Eye - Knee

Colombia

Pronunciation

Tay Ah-moe

Congo

Pronunciation

Sheh Tehm

Cyprus

Pronunciation

Shay Ah-gah-poe

Czech Republic

Pronunciation

Me-Lucy Chay

Denmark

Pronunciation

Yie Hoe-ler Ah-die

Ecuador

Pronunciation

Tay Ah-moe

Egypt

Ahna heh-Beck

Fiji

Pronunciation

May Ahp-co Bah-hoot
Bay-all Carta-hoom

Finland

Pronunciation

Min-neh Rock-ah-stah
Sin-you-ah

France

Pronunciation

Sheh Tehm

Gambia

I Love You

Germany

Eeek Leebah Deek

Ghana

Pronunciation

Me Doe Woo

Greece

Pronunciation

Shay Ah-gah-poe

Haiti

Pronunciation

Sheh Tehm

Honduras

Pronunciation

Tay Ah-moe

Hong Kong

Know - Oy - Lay

Hungary

Pronunciation

Sair-ret Lehk

India

Pronunciation

May Ahp-co Bah-hoot
Bay-all Carta-hoom

Indonesia

Pronunciation

Ah-koo Seen-tah Kah-moo

Iran

Mahn Ah-she-g Tow-ahm

Iraq

Pronunciation

Ahna heh-Beck

Ireland

Taw Graw Ah-gum Let

Israel

Pronunciation

Ah-knee Oh-hay-v
Oh-tawk-<u>h</u>

Italy

Pronunciation

Tee Ah-moe

Jamaica

Pronunciation

I Love You

Japan

Pronunciation

I She-tay E-rue

Jordan

Pronunciation

Ahna heh-Beck

Kenya

Pronunciation

Nah-coo-Pen-dah

Korea

Pronunciation

Sah Lawn-g
Hum Knee Dah

Kuwait

Ahna heh-Beck

Laos

Pronunciation

Coy Hawk Jaw-oh

Latvia

Pronunciation

Ehs Teh-vee Me-lou

Lebanon

Pronunciation

Ahna heh-Beck

Liberia

I Love You

Libya

Pronunciation

Ahna heh-Beck

Liechtenstein

Pronunciation

Eeek Leebah Deek

Lithuania

Pronunciation

Ahs me-Lou Teh-vee

Luxembourg

Pronunciation

Sheh Tehm

Macedonia

Pronunciation

Tay Sock-am

Malaysia

Pronunciation

Ah-koo Kah-say
Bah-dah Moo

Mali

Pronunciation

Sheh Tehm

Mexico

Tay Ah-moe

Monaco

Sheh Tehm

Morocco

Pronunciation

Ahna heh-Beck

Mozambique

Pronunciation

Ay-oh Ah-moe Voe-say

Netherlands

Pronunciation

Ick How Fawn Yow

New Zealand

Pronunciation

I Love You

Nigeria

Pronunciation

May See Ley Yow

Norway

Pronunciation

Yie Elsker Die

Panama

Pronunciation

Tay Ah-moe

Peru

Pronunciation

Tay Ah-moe

Philippines

Pronunciation

Mah-hal Kit-tah

Poland

Pronunciation

Cock-em Chell

Portugal

Ay-oh Ah-moe Voe-say

Rumania

Pronunciation

Teh You Bay-sk

Russia

Pronunciation

Ya Tib-ya Lou-blue

Rwanda

Pronunciation

Nah-coo-Pen-dah

Saudi Arabia

Pronunciation

Ahna heh-Beck

Singapore

Woll - Eye - Knee

Somalia

Pronunciation

Ooh-wan Coo Chet-la-high

Spain

Pronunciation

Tay Ah-moe

Sudan

Ahna heh-Beck

Sweden

Ya Elsker Day

Switzerland

Pronunciation

Eeek Leebah Deek

Syria

Pronunciation

Ahna heh-Beck

Tahiti

Pronunciation

Ooh-ah Hay-ray
Wow Ee-ah Oh-ah

Taiwan

Pronunciation

Woll - Eye - Knee

Tanganiers

Pronunciation

Nah-coo-Pen-dah

Thailand

Pronunciation

Pom Lock Koon

Tunisia

Pronunciation

Ahna heh-Beck

Turkey

Sen-yee Say-vee-your-rum

Uganda

I Love You

Ukraine

Pronunciation

Ya Lou-blue Teh-beh

United States

Pronunciation

I Love You

Venezuela

Pronunciation

Tay Ah-moe

Vietnam

Pronunciation

Ehm ewe Ahn

Yemen

Pronunciation

Ahna heh-Beck

Zaire

Pronunciation

Sheh Tehm
